Editor
Mara Ellen Guckian

Editorial Project Manager
Ina Massler Levin, M.A.

Editor in Chief
Sharon Coan, M.S. Ed.

Illustrator
Blanca Apodaca

Cover Artist
Sue Fullam

Art Coordinator
Denice Adorno

Creative Director
Elayne Roberts

Imaging
Ralph Olmedo, Jr.

Product Manager
Phil Garcia

Publishers
Rachelle Cracchiolo, M.S. Ed.
Mary Dupuy Smith, M.S. Ed.

Write a Story

Grades 1–3

Author

Kathleen Christopher Null

Teacher Created Materials, Inc.
6421 Industry Way
Westminster, CA 92683
www.teachercreated.com

©1999 Teacher Created Materials, Inc.
Reprinted, 2000

Made in U.S.A.
ISBN-1-57690-495-4

Table of Contents

Introduction

Stories have existed for as long as mankind. They have been passed on for generations and have benefited us all not only as entertainment but as life's lessons as well. A child whose life is enhanced by stories is rich indeed. Stories contribute to language acquisition, cultural heritage, relationships, and even brain development. Children have a natural affinity for stories. They love to hear them and tell them. If they can also love to write them, they will experience the academic advantages and pleasures of a lifelong heritage.

This book will introduce your students to the process of writing and enjoying stories. The first few pages contain the basics to assist you with beginning writers. From there, the book progresses into the specifics, beginning with some early story-structure experiences in the section titled "Story Structure" beginning on page 10.

Next you will find a section titled "Thinking Creatively" on page 16. You may use this section as an introduction, or you may use it at any time for the creative exercises.

"Plot," beginning on page 23, is a section that gives students some visual references for creating a plot with a conflict.

The "Essentials" section, page 28, covers the important elements of characterization, setting, the senses, and dialogue in stories.

More advanced essentials can be found in the "Tools" section beginning on page 36. This section discusses showing (as opposed to telling) point of view, metaphors, and similes.

In the "Time to Write" section beginning on page 41, students are guided in the writing process from the first draft (or "sloppy copy") to the writer's workshop to revision. There are some story starters to inspire students and information about publishing stories.

An answer key is included on page 48.

Though this book is designed to proceed in the order of the writing process, feel free to draw upon it whenever you wish. The activities are designed to also stand alone. Most of the activities include suggestions for modifying to fit the needs of younger students or to challenge more advanced students. You may wish to use some pages for class discussions by using an overhead or by passing out copies to students who can follow along.

This book is intentionally open-ended to allow you to incorporate the ideas as you see fit to meet particular students' needs. With the ideas in this book and your good ideas, your students will soon be enriched by the experience of writing their own stories, thereby gaining a greater appreciation for all literature.

What Is a Story?

A **story** is a tale. It can be told or it can be written. A story can be short, or it can be long. A story that is very long is called a novel. A story can be true (nonfiction) or made up (fiction).

> **Real or true stories** (nonfiction) can be found in magazines or books, and they can be in the form of biographies (stories about people) or true adventures.
>
> **Realistic stories** (fiction) are stories that tell about someone or something, and they seem real. They can be found in historical and adventure novels.
>
> **Fantasy stories** (fiction) are stories about characters and places that are not like anyone or anyplace you have ever known. These would include tall tales, fairy tales, science fiction, and, of course, stories about talking animals who do amazing things!

A story is a work of art that has been carefully planned by the author. You know when you read a good story. It makes you think, learn, laugh, cry, feel glad, feel sad, feel afraid, or just feel really good.

You have probably already written and told many stories. A story usually has the following parts:

- a beginning, a middle, and an ending
- two or three characters, but sometimes more
- descriptions of the characters and the setting
- use of the five senses
- expressions of feelings
- dialogue
- a problem
- a solution for the problem

Now it's time to think of all the stories you have read and those you have written. On the back of this page, write all the titles you can think of. Include the titles of stories that you or your friends have written. Here are some to get you started: *The Three Little Pigs*, *Where the Wild Things Are*, *Goodnight Moon*, and *Cinderella*. You will probably be surprised at how many you can think of.

Challenge: Have students organize the story titles they write into genres such as tall tales, fairy tales, adventures, etc.

For Younger Students: Make this a whole class activity and allow students to name the stories they think of as you write the titles on the board. This will also introduce the class to the concept of brainstorming.

4

Definitions

Here is a list of words that are used in this book. These are words that authors use in storywriting.

antagonist—The *antagonist* in a story is the "bad guy" or villain. An antagonist can also be a thing such as bad weather. An antagonist gets in the way of the hero or heroine in a story.

autobiography—An *autobiography* is a true story you write about yourself.

biography—A *biography* is a true story you write about someone else.

brainstorming—When you are *brainstorming*, you list every thought or idea that comes to you about your topic.

characters—The *characters* are the people or animals in a story.

conclusion—The *conclusion* occurs at the end of the story when the problem is solved and everyone is ready to live happily ever after.

conflict—A *conflict* is a problem in the story that needs to be solved.

description—Words and sentences that show what characters and settings look like, smell like, taste like, etc., are called *descriptions*.

dialogue—*Dialogue* is the words the characters in a story say to each other.

draft—A *draft* is a written version of the story. It may be a "sloppy copy" or the final draft.

editing—When *editing*, you carefully read a draft and make changes in words or grammar so that it sounds better.

fantasy—A made-up story is a *fantasy*. Fantasies often have strange settings and unusual characters.

fiction—*Fiction* is a made-up story, but it could be based on truth.

metaphor—A *metaphor* is created when one thing is compared to another, such as, "You're a grumpy bear today!"

narration—A *narration* tells something about a character or something that has happened in the story.

nonfiction—Stories and books that are true are *nonfiction*.

Definitions (cont.)

novel—A long work of fiction, such as a chapter book, is called a *novel*.

plot—The *plot* describes the action of the story. It is how one event follows another in order until the story ends.

point of view—The *point of view* is the opinion of the person telling the story.

protagonist—The hero, main character, or "good guy" is the *protagonist*. A *protagonist* is the opposite of an antagonist.

publish—When you *publish* your work, you share your written work with others in some form.

revise—When you *revise* your work, you make changes that will improve your story.

senses—The five *senses* are sight, touch, taste, smell, and hearing.

setting—The *setting* is where and when the story happens.

simile—A *simile* compares one thing to something else with words such as *like or as*. (Example: "You're as tiny as a mouse!")

slice of life—A *slice of life* is a very short story that is about what is seen, heard, felt, etc. in one moment.

sloppy copy—A *sloppy copy* is a term for a first draft that has not been corrected or edited.

story maps—*Story maps,* or plans, are a way to see what happens in a story.

style—The *style* or manner in which the story is written can be funny, scary, suspenseful, etc.

theme—The main idea of the story is its *theme*.

topic sentence—A *topic sentence* tells what the paragraph will be about.

writer's workshop—A group of writers who get together to help each other with their stories is called a *writer's workshop*.

Writing Well

Your most important job as a writer is to write clearly. Your ideas may be creative and wonderful, but they will be lost if your writing is too complicated or too fancy.

Here are some tips:

- **The most important words are nouns and verbs.** Nouns are persons, places or things (your friend, the mountain, and the sandwich in your lunch). Verbs are action words (jump, scream, sleep, or eat). You need nouns and verbs to write and speak in complete sentences. It's best to use specific nouns and verbs in order to paint a picture or tell a story. Use specific verbs to describe action.

For example, instead of writing,

She was really afraid.

write,

Lindsay's heart was pounding so hard she was sure the stranger would hear it!

Lindsay's and *pounding* indicate a specific person and a specific action.

- **Write every day**. Set a daily goal of 50 or 100 words. Write in a journal, a diary, or wherever you wish, but write daily. Remember, practice makes perfect.

- **Try learning to type.** The word processor can be a writer's best friend.

- **Keep a dictionary nearby and use it.**

- **Rewrite! Rewrite! Rewrite!** Learn to rewrite to find the clearest way to express your ideas and thoughts.

- **Read your writing aloud**. If you read your work aloud to family, friends, pets, or stuffed animals, it will become more clear to you whether or not you are making sense.

- **Read! Read! Read!** Read anything and everything, but especially read the work of good writers. Reading will strengthen your writing muscles!

The Writing Process

There are many steps that writers take to get from an idea to a story. You will take many steps, too. Sometimes you may repeat a step or even go backwards for a step or two. Here is a list of the kinds of steps you will go through.

Prewriting

During this step you will think about what you want to write about. To get ideas you can look at pictures, read books, brainstorm (see page 18), make lists, talk to people, sit and think, doodle, etc. You might also want to do some writing during this step to plan an idea, draw a setting, or describe how a character looks.

Incubation

During this step you will let your ideas rest and grow. You might want to take a break from your story idea and do something else for awhile. While you are doing something else, your brain will continue to work on your idea. When you go back to your story, you will have some more ideas about what to write.

First Draft

Finally, it's time to write your story. Don't try to write a perfect, finished story now. Just be creative and let the story come out. Don't stop to make corrections.

Editing

Now that you have had time to be a creative writer, it's time to be an editor. When you are editing your work, check it for spelling, punctuation, and the right words. Make sure you are making sense and saying what it is that you want to say.

8

The Writing Process *(cont.)*

Response/Writer's Workshop

In this step, you will get to see what someone else thinks about what you wrote. In a writer's workshop, you will hear from several of your classmates. Other ways to find out what others think is to ask friends, parents, and teachers to read your work and tell you what they think. When others are telling you what they think of your story, listen carefully. If they don't understand what you are saying, you will know that you need to make some changes, and they may have some suggestions for making your story more clear. You don't need to do as everyone suggests, but you will find some good advice that you will want to follow.

Revision

In this step, you will carefully think about what others have said, and you will make any changes that will make your story better. Rewrite your story as you wish, taking good ideas which were given to you. When you are finished, you will have another completed draft.

Evaluation

All writers experience some kind of evaluation. It might be the grade you get on your story, it might be what your classmates tell you about your story, or it might be what you think of it. When writers send their stories to publishers, the stories are evaluated in many ways as editors decide whether to publish them or not.

Publishing

Once your story is written in a form that can be read by others and others have read it, it has been published. If it is on the Internet, in a class book, posted on the bulletin board, or mailed to your pen pal, it is published. If you would like to have your story read by even more people, you can send it to a publication that uses the work of student writers (see page 47 for more information).

Beginnings, Middles, and Endings

All stories have a beginning, a middle, and an ending. Cut out the strips below and mix them up. See if you can arrange them into stories of three strips each.

Beginnings:

A little girl is sent to deliver lunch to her grandmother.
Elise wants a piano more than anything in the world, but her parents can't afford one.
Timmy is afraid to fly in an airplane, and his family is going to fly to his uncle's house in the summer.
Maria's sister keeps messing up the room they share no matter how much Maria asks her to be neat.
Daniel has no friends, and he really wants someone to play with at recess.
Kelli has to give a speech in class, and she is really afraid.

Middles:

She must walk through the forest. Along the way, she meets a wolf who asks her where she is going.
She writes a letter that explains that she would like a piano and that she would knit a blanket or sweater to trade for the piano. She sends the letter to everyone she knows, including all her relatives.
His grandpa takes him to the airport to talk to the people there. When the workers are not busy, they explain to him about how an airplane flies, how the seat belts work, and what they serve for snacks. One day, a pilot even lets Timmy and his grandpa look inside the cockpit and sit in a passenger seat.
She figures out that her sister has never learned how to be neat, so she tells her that she will give her lessons. After each lesson, she gives her sister a sticker.
He decides to ask his dad about how to make friends. His dad tells him to "be a friend" by being nice to others and to ask them to join him in a game.
She spends a lot of time writing her speech, and then she practices in front of the mirror. Next, she practices her speech in front of her family.

Beginnings, Middles, and Endings *(cont.)*

Endings:

When she gets to her grandmother's house, she discovers that it's not her grandmother at all, but the wolf! A woodsman hears them, comes to rescue her, and lets her grandmother out of the closet where she has been hiding, safe and sound.
She waits for so long that she is certain she will never have a piano. Then one day, she receives a letter from her grandmother saying that she is not using her piano anymore and will gladly trade it for a lap blanket and wonders if Elise can knit one in blue for her.
When his family finally goes to the airport, they are surprised to see so many airport workers saying "Hi" to Timmy. They are also surprised when Timmy walks on board with a smile on his face. When they wave good-bye to grandpa, they wonder why he is winking at Timmy.
One day, she comes home and finds that the entire room has been cleaned up by her sister. There is one little mess on the floor where her sister is putting all of her stickers into a scrapbook.
The next day at school he tells Tran that he really likes his book report and asks if he would like to play kickball with him. Tran is glad that he has a friend, and soon Daniel makes many more friends.
She practices so much that when she gets up in front of her class, she is only a little bit nervous at first, and soon it is easy. When she finishes, she sighs and smiles.

Challenge: Using a plot from a set of strips, write the entire story, including what the characters say to each other.

For Younger Students: Give students the beginning and middle strips and have them find the ending that matches. Also have them find a match when they have the middle and ending or the beginning and ending.

Paragraph Writing

Just like a story, a paragraph has a beginning, a middle, and an ending. The beginning tells what the paragraph will be about. The first sentence of the paragraph is called the **topic sentence** because it tells what the topic will be.

The middle of the paragraph is where you will find the sentences that say more about the topic. These sentences are called **supporting sentences**.

The **ending** of a paragraph is the last sentence or two. In the ending you tell the final details, give a summary, or make your point.

Here is a paragraph that has been taken apart so you can see how the parts fit together.

Topic Sentence:	Living on a boat would be a really good idea.
Supporting Sentences:	I could catch my dinner just by fishing off the side. The rocking boat would rock me to sleep at night. If I wanted to go somewhere, I could just hoist the sail and go. I could go swimming almost anytime I wanted to.
Ending:	It would be so great to be able to catch my own fish, to be rocked to sleep at night, to be able to swim and sail anytime I wanted to. It would be great to live on a boat.

Challenge: Write a paragraph about another place you would like to live. Write a topic sentence, supporting sentences, and a conclusion.

For Younger Students: Enlarge the sample paragraph, or copy it to use on an overhead projector. Read the paragraph all the way through without stopping. Discuss how the middle sentences support the topic sentence. Discuss how the concluding sentences sum up the body sentences.

▲▽ ▲▽ ▲▽ ▲▽ ▲▽ ▲▽ ▲▽ ▲▽ ▶

A Slice of Life

If you could reach out and grab a piece of life that you could hold onto and look at, you would have "a slice of life." A slice of life is like a snapshot that you write. Sometimes it is called a "vignette" (vin-yet). Whatever it is called, it is a short piece of writing that describes the senses and setting of a moment. It has no beginning, and it has no ending. Look around you right now. What do you see? Who do you see? What do you smell, taste, touch, and hear? If you wrote the answers to all of those questions right now, you would be writing a slice of life, or a vignette. Choose one of the assignments (1–3) on this page and the next and try writing a "snapshot" yourself.

1. Take a piece of paper and go into a room where there are two or more people. Write what you see and who you see. Describe them and what they are doing. Write down any sounds you hear, and describe smells, too. Write everything you can observe with the senses, and also write about what the mood is, if you can tell. Write what people say. Fill up the page with everything you can see, hear, touch, taste, and smell.

Here is an example to get you started.

> The lights are so bright that students squint as they come inside from the rainy day. There is rustling as students take off raincoats, and there are funny floppy sounds as rain boots fall to the floor. They sit on the rug near the piano and Mrs. Griffiths begins to play some soft, tinkling music. There is the smell of wet wool. Some students are scratching where their wool sweaters itch them. Soon all students are seated on the pale, rose-colored carpet. There is some giggling and sniffing, and then Mrs. Griffiths stands up. There is a whoosh as all the students stand for the Pledge of Allegiance.

2. Find some old magazines and cut out pictures of people and places. Put the people pictures in one envelope and the place pictures in another. Reach into the people envelope and pull out two people (no peeking!). Take one picture from the place envelope. Now take out a piece of paper and make up a "snapshot" story about the people and place. The following paragraph is a part of one student's work. The pictures she used were of a funny-looking lady with a head full of pink curlers, a very dirty little boy, and a kitchen. (See example next page.)

A Slice of Life *(cont.)*

Benjamin tracked mud across his grandmother's kitchen and reached for a glass of milk on the edge of the counter. He slurped milk noisily and then tried to put the glass into the sink. Suddenly, realizing that someone was watching him, he shrieked and dropped the glass. He had never seen anyone with pink things all over her head before. The glass broke, and then he looked down and saw the mud all over the floor and his shoes. He looked up at his grandmother and said, "I...um...." His grandmother interrupted, "What do you say we go get some ice cream after we clean up this mess?" Benjamin laughed out loud, hugged his grandmother, and then asked, "And what about the mess on your head, Grandma?"

3. Cut out the settings and characters below and mix them up. Put the choices in a hat or box and choose, without looking, two characters and one setting. Write a slice-of-life story using the characters and the place that you have picked.

Characters

a babysitter	a puppy	a stuffed animal
a teacher	a dad	a monster
an artist	a clown	a nurse

Settings

a playground	a classroom	an island
a campground	a store	a beach

Challenge: In a vignette notebook, write vignettes in busy places (airports, markets, schools) and quiet places (libraries, churches).

For Younger Students: Write a group "slice-of-life" piece on the board with students contributing what they observe with their senses (an airplane flying overhead, a bell, students in the next classroom, the smell of crayons, etc.).

Looking at Stories

Have you ever taken something apart to see how it was made or how it works? When Jason was a little boy, he took apart his shoes, a watch, and a radio. When his mom asked him why, he said he wanted to see how things were made and what made them work. Unless you know how to put it back together again, it is probably not a good idea to take a radio apart, but you can take a story apart to see how it works and how it was made. Here are some ways:

1. **Story Map.** After you read a story, draw a story map. Here is a story map for *Goldilocks and the Three Bears.*

2. **Visual Look at Your Story.** Choose a story and count how many paragraphs or

pages are in the story. Make the same number of squares on a large sheet of paper. Make the squares large enough for you to draw in them. Draw in the squares to make a cartoon strip of your story.

3. **Written Look at Your Story.** Take a piece of paper for each paragraph or page of your story. Number the pieces of paper. On each piece of paper, write what happens in each paragraph or on each page. Don't copy the words, just briefly write in your own words. For example, using the *Goldilocks* story, your work might look something like this:

   Page 1—Mama Bear, Papa Bear, and Baby Bear are sitting down at the table, getting ready to eat their porridge.

   Page 2—Papa Bear says that his porridge is too hot. Mama Bear says that hers is too cold, and Baby Bear says that his is just right.

   Page 3—Papa Bear says that they will go take a walk while their porridge cools.

4. **Mixed-up Story.** Make a copy of your favorite story. Cut the paragraphs apart. Mix them up. See if you can put them back together again in the right order.

Be Creative!

Creative writing needs creative thinking. Here are some ways to be a more creative thinker.

1. **Ask lots of questions:**
   - Why do cats meow?
   - Why is the earth round?
   - How do kites fly?
   - Why do telephones ring?
   - Who invented music?

   Can you think of five more questions?

2. **Ask "what if" questions:**
   - What if dogs could fly?
   - What if snowmen could talk?
   - What if we traded places with our parents?
   - What if none of us had any hair at all?
   - What if we all had to go everywhere on roller blades?

   Ask five more "what if" questions.

3. **Look at the pictures below. For each one, name as many things as you can think of that you could do with each item.** How many can you think of? Just a few? Hundreds? If you want to think of more, try to look at the objects as being whatever size you want and in any position you can imagine. For instance, the box could be a house, a car, a hat, a bed, a dress, a matchbox, a television set, a bus, a building, or a robot if you add a couple of things here and there.

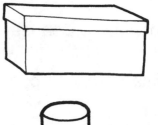 =  **or**

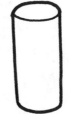 =  **or**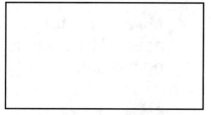

16

Be Creative! *(cont.)*

To increase your creativity, try some modification (ma-da-fi-KAY-shun)! Modification is when you take something that already exists and make it into something new by changing it. When you write stories you often take something that is real (your school) and modify it to make a new story (your school as a spaceship). Using the figures below, draw (or modify) to make the lines into pictures. When you are finished, you can compare your pictures with your classmates' drawings.

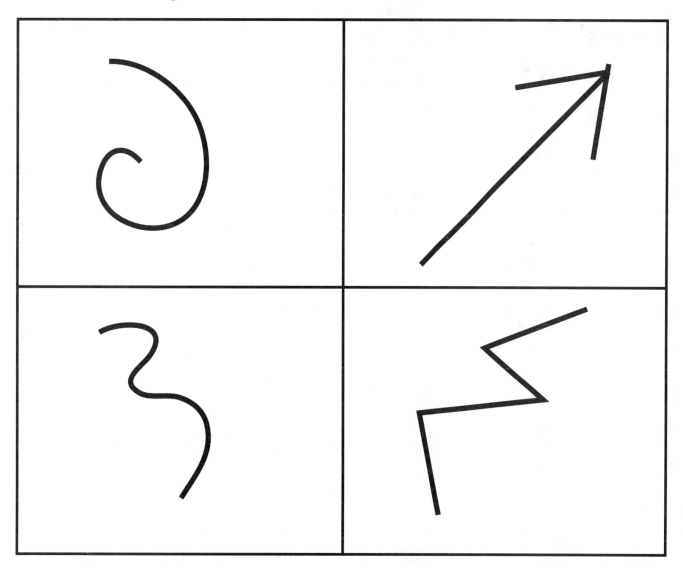

Challenge: Create six doodles and trade them with your classmates. Try making a different drawing for each doodle. Also, try making one big drawing by using all the doodles on the page. Do some doodling each time you write as a warm-up for your creativity.

A Storm in Your Brain!

When you start thinking of lots of ideas, you are brainstorming. When you brainstorm, don't stop to think about whether your ideas are good or not, just write them all down. You can brainstorm alone or with others. To try brainstorming alone, pick one of the ideas from the list below. Write the idea in the circle. Then, think of everything and anything that comes to your mind about this topic. Write everything you think of in the box around the circle. Don't worry if some of your ideas seem silly or not "correct." Just write down everything, and don't stop until you are sure you have run out of ideas.

- candy
- yellow things
- summer

- my grandma
- merry-go-rounds
- sports

- food
- sticky things
- pets

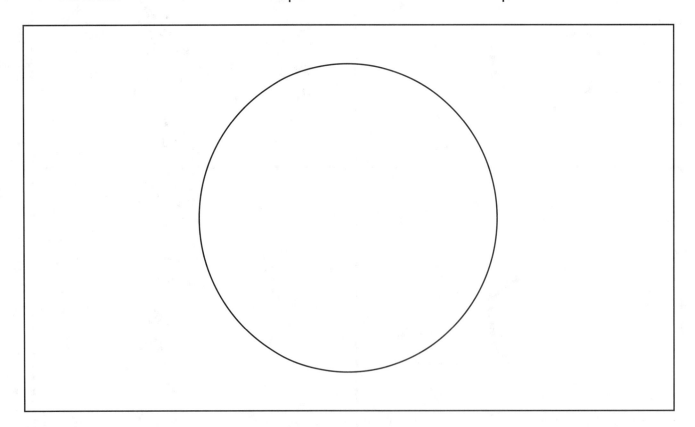

Challenge: After you have finished brainstorming, circle the ideas you like best, and write a story using your topic and your ideas.

For Younger Students: Demonstrate brainstorming on the board by choosing one of the topics, or one of your own, encouraging students to call out their ideas while you write them. Be sure to avoid judging any of the responses.

What Did You Dream?

Once I dreamed that there was a castle in my backyard and no one could see it but me. I went inside and found it was full of toys and my favorite foods. I was busy eating marshmallows when my brother woke me up to tell me I was chewing on my pillow!

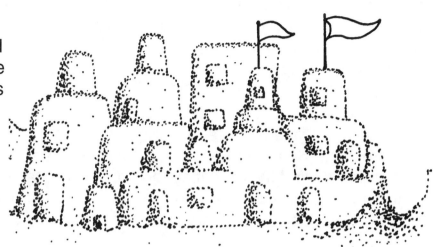

Describe a dream that you once had and draw a picture to go with it.

_____

_____

_____

Team Stories

Have you ever made up stories with your friends with each of you taking a turn to add to the story? It can be fun to add your part to a story that is written by a team of writers.

Here is how to do it with your whole class:

1. Take out a piece of paper. Your teacher will give you some time to write a one-page or one-paragraph beginning to a story. Think of ways to make it interesting. Be sure to write about a character or two and a place for the characters. Will they be at school, on a mountain trail, on another planet, or at home? Be creative and think of the most interesting characters you can. Put the characters in a very interesting place. Add a title at the top of the story.

2. When you have finished, look carefully to make sure other people will be able to read what you wrote.

3. Your teacher will stop you when the time is up. Stop and turn in your story start.

4. After all the story starts are collected, your teacher will collect them and make copies.

5. Next, your teacher will pass out the story starts (maybe on another day). You should have one that someone else wrote. If you get your own, be sure to let your teacher know.

6. You will have time to write the middle part of someone else's story now. Be sure to use the same characters that are in the beginning of the story and decide how it will continue.

7. Check to make sure your middle can be read by others and turn it in. Your teacher will copy the new, longer stories.

8. Finally, it will be time to write the endings to the stories. Your teacher will pass out the stories again. Be sure that you get a story that was written by others and not you.

9. Now you have the tough job of writing an ending to a story that you did not start. Be sure to use the same characters and write an ending that makes sense.

10. Your teacher will collect all of the stories. Soon you will have a story festival, sharing the team stories.

Team Stories *(cont.)*

The Story Festival

Your teacher will state the title of the first story to be read. The author of that story's beginning will come up to read the whole story. When you hear the title you wrote, you will go to the front of the class to read your team's story. You may be surprised at what happened to your story. When you finish reading the whole story, you may wish to tell the class how you thought the story would go and what surprised you about the middle and ending.

When everyone is finished, discuss the stories. Did anyone have trouble continuing a story? Why? Did any story come out just as expected? What were you thinking or feeling as you were writing your story parts? Which was the most fun: the beginning, the middle, or the ending? Which was the easiest to write?

Challenge: In a report folder with about 10 pages, write a story start on the first page. Add your name to the bottom of the page. Put your folder in a box or on a shelf with the story folders of the rest of the class. When you have some free time, take out another folder, add a page to whatever story had been started, and add your name to the bottom of that page. Don't write your pages one after another; be sure to allow someone else a turn in between. You can write in as many books as you like, however. If you want, you can add an illustration to your page. Don't forget to read the stories too.

For Younger Students: Have the class, or a team of students, sit in a circle. Allot a time period, and pick a number so that students can try to guess the number. The student who comes closest gets to begin. The first student starts the story by introducing the characters and the setting, begins to tell some of the action, and then stops. The student to his or her left takes up where the first student left off and stops to allow the next student to continue, and so on. Continue as many times around the circle as time allows. (If you use a timer, let students see how much time is left, and it may motivate them to start tying together loose ends to create a conclusion.)

Team Stories *(cont.)*

Here are some story starters to help you.

Tomas ran home from school as fast as he could. He wanted to watch his favorite show. When he got inside the house, his brother, Hector, was standing in front of the TV. "I think you better take care of something first," he said. "What?" Tomas asked, trying to get around his brother. "Go look at Rexie," Hector said. Tomas went into the backyard and whistled for his big white dog, Rexie. Rexie came running around the corner, but he wasn't white anymore. He was green!

When Meagan woke up, she rubbed her eyes and stumbled into the kitchen to find something to eat. After she ate, she looked around the house. There was no radio on, no TV on, and her brother, Jeffrey, was not taking a shower. It was really quiet. "Where is everybody?" she said.

After getting off the Ferris wheel, Kyle and Cori went to get some cotton candy. Their parents were going to meet them by the pony rides, where their little sister, Eliza, wanted to go for a ride. As they were getting their cotton candy, they argued about who should pay. Kyle owed Cori $2.00, and he hadn't paid her yet. They argued all the way to the pony rides. They stopped because they didn't want to go home yet. They looked around and didn't see their parents or Eliza anywhere. On a bench they found three packages, and they each had Cori's name on them.

Sarah put her stuffed animals and dolls carefully on the shelf each night before she went to bed. Then her mom read her a bedtime story. After the story, Sarah said to her mom, "I think my animals and dolls get up and play when I'm asleep." Her mom said, "I don't think they would do that." Sarah decided to look very carefully at her toys before she turned off the light. The next morning she looked at them, and she was sure they had moved.

What Is This Story About?

The **theme** is the meaning in a story. In the story *Little Red Riding Hood,* the little girl must be brave when she goes through the forest and when she finds the wolf in her grandmother's bed. The story has a happy ending, and the little girl and the grandmother never become dinner for the wolf. The theme of this story is that it is good to be brave and that good things happen to brave people. In *The Three Little Pigs,* the pig who prepares and builds his house of brick is the one able to escape the wolf. The theme of this story might be that it is wise to be prepared.

Here are some more stories. Put an **X** by the theme that you think best fits each story.

Cinderella	_____ It's a good idea to have pumpkins around. _____ Goodness brings the best things in life. _____ People should be nice to mice.
Beauty and the Beast	_____ Don't judge a book by its cover. _____ It's a good idea to know how to dance. _____ Might makes right.
Pinocchio	_____ The early bird catches the worm. _____ It's important to be prepared. _____ Honesty is the best choice.

Challenge: Choose one of these themes and write a story to illustrate it.

- Honesty is the best policy.
- Money is not everything.
- Crime does not pay.
- Don't judge a book by its cover.

For Younger Students: Use this page for discussion with an overhead projector or on the board. Introduce the concept of themes as underlying and/or unifying meaning. Perhaps the topic of birthday party themes might help introduce this topic (for instance, a space theme throughout a party's decor, favors, cake, etc.) As a class, discuss the theme choices for the stories listed and which choice makes the best theme. Explain how authors can express the theme, "honesty is important" through a story.

A Plot Is Like a Map

A **plot** is a plan for your story. The plot is what happens in the story. You have used plots before. Here is an example of a plot in the words of Kevin:

"When we first got there, we ran to get on Space Mountain. We didn't have to wait too long, and then we went to Indiana Jones. We had to wait a long time then, but Lan kept telling us all the jokes he knows so we were all laughing. Next we went to eat French fries with lots of ketchup, and we watched the river boats while we ate. We decided to go on Splash Mountain after that, but when we got there it was closed. It had broken down. We asked how long it would be, and the man said it would be about an hour. This made us mad because we wanted to get wet right away. Instead, we went to ride the tea cups. Jaime got sick and threw up in the bushes! It was so embarrassing. We laughed, but Jaime wasn't laughing. In fact, Jaime didn't want to do anything after that, not even Splash Mountain. We sat around and then just went home early."

Kevin's story tells what happens first, what happens next, and what happens after that. He also tells about a problem that happened (Jaime got sick) and what they did about it (went home).

When you are writing a story, it's a good idea to first write a plot outline so you won't get lost or forget what you wanted to say. Here is an example of a plot outline:

1. A girl finds a puppy in the park. She takes it home and wishes she could keep it because it is so cute.

2 She sees it has a tag with an address nearby. She decides that someone is probably sad and missing the puppy.

3. She and her dad take it to the address and find a boy who has been crying. The boy and the puppy are happy to see each other again.

When your plot outline is finished, add details to each part to finish your story.

A Plot Is Like a Map *(cont.)*

Read the plot outlines below. Put the events in the order (1–3) they should happen.

Fairy Tale Plot

_____Her fairy godmother rescues her and sends her to the ball.

_____The wicked stepsisters prevent her from going to the ball.

_____The prince finds her when her foot fits the glass slipper.

Adventure Plot

_____They get to go on their adventure. They have a great time!

_____They recycle lots of newspapers, cans, and bottles.

_____The class wants to take a hot air balloon trip, but it will cost a lot of money.

You may have noticed that the plot is just one of the three most important parts of your story. You need a setting, characters, and a plot.

1. The **setting** is where and when the story happens.

2. The **characters** are the people or animals that the story is about.

3. The **plot** is what happens in the story. It is how one event follows another in order until the story ends.

The plot is important. It introduces the character in a setting and then shows the reader that the character has a problem. The plot is what happens as the character tries to solve the problem and how he or she finally finds a solution. In "Cinderella" the problem is that she wants to go to the ball. The wicked stepmother and sisters are also a problem. The fairy godmother makes it possible for her to go to the ball and to meet the prince. The solution is that he finds her and marries her, and the wicked stepmother and sisters don't bother her anymore.

Challenge: Take one of the plot outlines above (or from page 24), or make up one of your own, and fill in the details, including what the characters say to each other. Keep adding until you have written a story. Take some favorite stories and write different endings for them.

We Need a Bad Guy!

If you want to write an interesting story that will have your friends eager to read what happens next, you will need a bad guy and a problem or a conflict. Without a problem, there will be nothing for your main character to do. Without a problem, your story will be boring because nothing will be happening.

Your main character is the "good guy." He or she is also called a **protagonist**.

The problem is the "bad guy," or villain, which can be an animal, a snowstorm, or anything you can think of that will slow down or threaten your "good guy."

The bad guy, or the problem, is called the **antagonist**.

See if you can think of who the bad guy, or antagonist, is in each of these stories. The first one has been completed for you.

Protagonist (Good Guy)	Antagonist (Bad Guy)
The Three Little Pigs Cinderella Sleeping Beauty 101 Dalmatians Hansel and Gretel Little Red Riding Hood	the wolf

Challenge: On a separate piece of paper, list a possible **antagonist** (villain, problem, or obstacle) for each of these **protagonists**: a basketball star, a cat, an old man, a bird, a mailman, a policeman, a seven-year-old boy or girl, an astronaut.

For Younger Students: As a class, brainstorm a story setting and one or two characters. Write them on the board. Next, brainstorm the first obstacle for the main character(s) and then brainstorm possible solutions. (For instance, if the characters are confronted by a snarling dog, students may list possible solutions such as climbing a tree, donating lunch, hiding, etc.) Brainstorm the next obstacle and solution. Emphasize that there are many problems that we all confront each day, and so do the characters in stories.

Plot

How Will It End?

Problem solving is not easy for most of us. It's not easy for the characters in books either. When you read a book or see a movie where the character is in a lot of trouble, you want to keep reading or watching to find out how it will end. Here is a character who is in a lot of trouble:

A poor girl wants to go to the ball, but she has no way to get there, nothing pretty to wear, and she has too many chores to do. Her stepsisters do all they can to make her life miserable.

Those are just some of the problems that Cinderella has to solve.

There is more than one way to solve a problem and to end a story. Read this plot outline and get ready to write two different endings for the story.

Mike and Derek have been friends since they were little boys. Even though Mike has trouble talking, Derek has never had any trouble understanding him. When it is time for them to go to school, they plan to continue to be friends. At school many students tease Mike and say mean things about him. They tell Derek that if he is friends with Mike, they can't be friends with him. Derek has to make a choice. He can keep Mike as a friend and have no other friends, or he can stop being friends with Mike and be popular.

Ending 1

In the space below, write an ending where Derek chooses to end his friendship with Mike. Why does he decide this, and what happens?

_____

_____

_____

Ending 2

In the space below, write an ending where Derek chooses to keep his friendship with Mike. Why does he decide this, and what happens?

_____

_____

_____

© *Teacher Created Materials, Inc.* 27 *#2495 How to Write a Story*

What a Character!

The characters you make up for your stories will seem more real if they seem real to you. It is helpful to imagine a character and then really get to know him or her. One way to do this is to make up a profile for your character. You may use the form below or make up your own questions. After you know your character really well, you will know what he or she looks like and what he or she would do. Think of a character for your next story and answer the questions about him or her:

Name of Character _____

Age_____ Height_____ Weight_____ Male or Female_____

Hair Color_____ Eye Color_____ Skin Color _____

Where does he or she live?_____

What does he or she do each day (job, school, etc.)? _____

List the character's favorite: Color_____ Hobby _____

Food_____ Sport_____

Animal_____ Music_____ Book _____

Place to go_____ Movie _____

Thing to do on a rainy day_____

Thing to do on a sunny day_____

Best friend_____ Worst enemy _____

Personality (funny, serious, shy, bold, etc.) _____

Would you like to have this character as a friend? _____

Why or why not? _____

Challenge: Here are some other ways to get to know your character. Get an employment application (ask a parent or teacher), and fill it out as your character might. Have a friend interview you while you pretend to be your character. Answer all the questions as your character.

For Younger Students: Choose fictional characters who are familiar to your students. Have students pretend to be the characters (in turns) while the class asks questions of the character. As a class, fill in the profile using a familiar character.

All Set!

Have you ever seen a play on stage? If you have, you probably noticed that there was a set on the stage even before the actors went on stage. The **set** may have been of the inside of a house, an outdoor scene, or maybe even a circus. When you write a story, you need a set, too, for your characters. You won't need to build it with a hammer and nails, though. You will build it in your imagination and write it on paper. With stories, the set is called a **setting**. Sometimes it helps you write about your setting if you first draw what it looks like. Using a story that you want to write or a favorite story, draw a setting for it in the space below. Be sure to add color. Don't add the characters; only draw the setting. If you can't think of what to draw, choose one of these: the three bears' house, the forest through which Little Red Riding Hood had to walk, the inside of a spacecraft in which the Little Prince might travel, Sleeping Beauty's castle, or a pirate setting for the characters in *Treasure Island.*

It's Crunchy!

Your readers will have a lot more fun reading your stories if you include the five senses. They will feel like they are really there if they can see, smell, feel, taste, and hear everything in your story. A good way to think of all the different senses in a story is to use a sense matrix. Here is an example of a sense matrix. On page 31, you will find one to use for your stories.

SENSE MATRIX					
Setting	**Looks like**	**Feels like**	**Smells like**	**Tastes like**	**Sounds like**
Thanksgiving at Our House	orange and red leaves brown, juicy turkey orange pumpkin pie fluffy, white potatoes	crisp and cool crispy apples warm fire hugs	pumpkin pie turkey fireplace smoke	spicy warm yummy salty, sweet	voices in the kitchen cousins laughing crackling fire
The Lunch Area at School	chipped paint on the tables benches oily blacktop fries on the ground	hot in the sun elbows bumping milk carton is cold and beaded with water drops	fried food ketchup peanut butter	gooey cheese salty chips sweet cookies	a roar of voices crunching carrots teachers' whistles

It's Crunchy! *(cont.)*

My Setting _____

SENSE MATRIX				
Looks like	**Feels like**	**Smells like**	**Tastes like**	**Sounds like**

It's Crunchy! *(cont.)*

Have you ever read a story that took you somewhere far away? A good story uses the senses to make the reader feel like he or she is really there. Here's a challenge for you. Try writing one sentence for each of the five senses, according to the directions below. Write so that those who read your sentences will see, hear, smell, taste, or touch what you have described.

1. Write a sentence that shows what the ocean **looks** like. Do not use the words big, huge, or blue.

   _____

   _____

2. Write a sentence that shows what a cat's purr **sounds** like.

   _____

   _____

3. Write a sentence that shows how a flower **smells**. Do not use the words pretty or good.

   _____

   _____

4. Write a sentence that shows what chocolate **tastes** like. Do not use the words creamy, good, or sweet.

   _____

   _____

5. Write a sentence that shows how a snake **feels**. Do not use the words slimy or slithery.

   _____

   _____

Challenge: Keep a senses notebook with a section for each sense. When you find yourself waiting for someone or in a line, take it out and write descriptions of what you are observing, using the five senses.

For Younger Students: Make up or find some examples of creative descriptions using the senses. Share them with the students. Allow them to dictate responses to the five prompts. Encourage them to be original. You might want to write their responses on separate sheets of paper so they can illustrate them and have them stapled into a book.

Yakety-Yak!

When your characters start talking to each other, that is called **dialogue**. Dialogue helps you to show what a character is like.

If someone falls down and your character says, "Hah! That was pretty funny!" that tells the reader what your character is like. If instead your character says, "Are you okay?" that says something different about your character.

Imagine two characters. One is **nasty** and the other is **nice**. Below, write what each character might say in each of the situations.

	Nasty	Nice
To a new boy at school	"You can't play."	"Come play with us."
To someone who has just offered an invitation to a party		
To the substitute teacher		
To a parent who has said it's time for bed		
To the teacher who says it's time to put away the equipment		

Challenge: Listen to dialogue wherever you go. Listen to people of all ages in all kinds of places. Write down interesting sayings, expressions, or accents you hear. Using the activity above write the responses you might imagine from a timid character, a funny character, a smart character, or an athletic character.

For Younger Students: Take dictation as they think of how one type of person might respond as opposed to another: For instance, to the new boy in school, the nasty character might say, "Get lost," or "Go away!" The nice character might say, "Hello," or "Do you want to play with us?" Be sure they realize that this activity is not about any real person they know or themselves; it is about fictional characters that they are imagining.

Yakety-Yak! *(cont.)*

When you are in the room with someone who is talking on the telephone, all you hear is one side of the conversation. You have to use your imagination to think of what the other person might be saying. Here is one part of a conversation. Use your imagination to write what the other person might be saying. You can be as creative as you like, but make it sound like a real conversation when you finish.

"Hello."

_____

"I'm looking for a book about spiders."

_____

"Me too."

_____

"Do you like to read? I love to read."

_____

"Oh, I don't like that kind of book at all!"

_____

"Well, maybe."

_____

"I prefer books about people."

_____

"Okay, I will see you later!"

_____

"Bye!"

_____

Challenge: Write a one-page dialogue. Write it again on another piece of paper, only this time leave out one of the speakers so that only one-half of the dialogue appears on the paper. Leave spaces between each line of dialogue. Exchange papers (the page with only half of a dialogue) with class members. Try to fill in the spaces with what the other character might say. Read both the actual dialogues and the newly created dialogues in front of the class. Some should be really interesting, and some will be quite funny.

34

Yakety-Yak! *(cont.)*

Writing dialogue takes practice. The more you listen to people talking and the more you write dialogue, the better you will get. Write a dialogue for one of the following situations. Be sure to let both sides talk!

- Two friends are talking about why they do not like the dog down the street.

- A mother and child are talking about what time the child should go to bed.

- A boy is telling his babysitter that he can eat whatever he wants and the babysitter disagrees.

- Red Riding Hood and her mother are talking about what happened the day she went to her grandmother's.

- A father and child are talking about what to get at the grocery store.

- A bird and a worm are having an early-morning chat.

- A student is talking to the teacher about why his or her homework is not finished.

- The monster under the bed and the daddy who was just called into the room are having a conversation.

- Two friends are talking about why they like ice cream.

- Two strangers are having a conversation in an elevator at the airport.

Challenge: Look for stories containing paragraphs that describe what happens to the characters without using dialogue. Rewrite the paragraphs using dialogue instead. For example, you might find a paragraph that tells about how a family had to move because their house was slipping slowly down the hillside. Write a page of dialogue to show what the family members and others may have been saying to each other about this problem.

For Younger Students: Have students use the situations in the activity to role-play the characters talking to each other. Emphasize that what they are doing is having a dialogue. Read them examples of dialogue in their favorite books.

For Younger Students: Find some examples of dialogue from favorite books. Read to the students one-half of the conversation. Let them think about what might be said on the other side. Then read the complete dialogue. Did they have the right idea, or were they thinking of something else entirely? Using toy or nonfunctional telephones, have students take turns pretending to have a conversation.

Show Me

What if a strange space vehicle landed in your friend's backyard and instead of letting you come see it, he said to you, "I'll just tell you about it, and then you won't have to see it." How would you feel? Wouldn't you rather go see it yourself? Good writing lets the reader see it for him or herself. When someone writes, "There was a vase full of pretty flowers on the table," they are saying to you, the reader, "Trust me, I am telling you they were pretty. You won't need to see them for yourself, because I have told you they were pretty." That's not fair! Good writing doesn't tell; it shows. When it **shows**, the reader gets to make up his or her own mind.

Circle the sentences below that let you "see" what is described. **Underline** the sentences that make you wish you could just see it yourself. The first two have been completed for you.

1. <u>There was a vase full of pretty flowers on the table.</u>
2. There was a tall, blue vase full of bright, purple irises on the table.
3. Maria saw a dog.
4. Maria saw a tiny, white dog with muddy paws and a nervous tail.
5. Mr. Olsen is nice.
6. I saw Mr. Olsen buy lunch for Lanni after Joey sat on hers.
7. I live in a house.
8. That's a noisy car.
9. My cat sounds like an engine starting when she purrs.
10. My mom is a good cook.
11. There's a monster under my bed.
12. Her hair is the color of a tortilla before it is cooked.
13. My dad is a big man.
14. That car is the color of pistachio ice cream.

Challenge: Write at least one "showing" sentence to replace each "telling" sentence you found.

For Younger Students: Give them a subject to draw, such as the dog Maria saw in #2. Each student will draw a different dog because they have no description to let them "see" the dog that Maria saw. Discuss why they drew different dogs. Next, give them the description in #4 to draw. Although there will be variations, the students should have similar drawings because they were able to "see" the dog more specifically.

Different Ways of Seeing

The **point of view** is the place from which things are seen. If you climb up to the top of the highest tree in your neighborhood, you will have a very different view than your mom will as she stands on the ground and tries to get you to come down. You will see all the rooftops and streets and backyards in your neighborhood and some birds flying by at eye level. Your mom will see you as a tiny shape up in the tree branches, and she will be hoping that you don't slip and fall. You will be seeing things one way, and your mom will be seeing things another way. After you come down from the tree, you and your mom could write about what happened and have different stories. If you decide, later, to write a story about a boy or girl in a tree, you will need to decide from which point of view you will write your story.

Here are your choices:

1. **First Person Point of View:** The author is a character in the story. He is the "I" in the story. Here is an example:

   I always loved climbing that tree. I didn't know that it worried my mom because she was a tiny figure down below.

2. **Third Person Point of View:** The author tells the story without being a character in the story. The author is like a reporter telling the story. Here is an example:

   She always loved to climb that tree. She didn't know that it worried her mom because she only saw her tiny figure standing below.

3. **Omniscient Point of View:** The author can be anywhere and can tell the story from the point of view of any character. For example:

   He always loved to climb that tree. Below, his mother paced and clutched her hands together, fearful that he might slip and fall.

Challenge: Look inside several books to determine from which point of view they were written. You may need to read two or three pages to be sure. Make one stack for First Person, one for Third Person, one for Omniscient, and one for Don't Know. There are other points of view, but they are more rare. Which stack is the highest? The shortest?

For Younger Students: Make a chart that has headings for each point of view. From the children's reading, collect a few samples of each point of view to write in the appropriate columns. Have students find more and add them over a period of several weeks.

Different Ways of Seeing *(cont.)*

Take some paper and rewrite one of these stories from a different point of view.

The Gingerbread Man from the point of view of the fox

The Three Little Pigs from the point of view of the wolf

Goldilocks from the point of view of the baby bear

Little Red Riding Hood from the point of view of the grandmother

Challenge: Find a story and read it carefully to find its point of view. Rewrite it in third person if it is in first person or first person if it is in third person. Try rewriting one of your own stories from more than one point of view.

For Younger Students: Choose a story and, as a class, retell it orally with students offering their ideas. The wolf, for instance, in *Little Red Riding Hood* may have a different story to tell.

In Style!

Ten different writers might tell the same story, and it will sound a little different each time. Why? Because each writer will write in his or her own style. **Style** is how the author uses language. The author can also set a tone or mood with how he writes. He can write in a scary style, a happy style, a funny style, a sad style, or any style that can be imagined. There are many ways to write a story. Here are first lines from some stories. For each one, take out a piece of paper and draw a picture that matches the style of the story. If it sounds like a scary story, draw a scary picture, etc. Put a number 1–5 on each of your drawings and be prepared to share in class.

1. Cassie woke up, looked around her room, and saw lots of colorful balloons that made her smile.

2. They walked slowly through the dark forest, looking to the right and the left, quietly walking, holding onto each other, and trembling with fear.

3. I raced across the street while cars and taxis honked at me, and the kids in front of the school said, "There's that new kid from the country!"

4. Several people stood in the dark room, gathered around the place where the thief had cut the glass and stolen the school mascot.

5. Once upon a time there was a beautiful princess who lived in a castle overlooking a sparkling sea.

Challenge: Choose one of the opening lines above and finish the story.

For Younger Students: Give the students a familiar story, *Goldilocks* for instance, to write or tell in their own words. Discuss with the class how some people told it one way and others another way. Talk about the variations in the telling: the tone, the details, etc. Explain that even though the plot is the same, the differences are because of the different styles.

Life Is Like a Banana

When you say, "My brother is a toad!" you have just created a **metaphor**. A metaphor compares one thing to another by saying that the one thing is the other thing. Some more examples are:

- I am a hungry bear today!
- Watch out, she's a monster!

When you say, "My best friend is as tiny as a mouse," you have created a **simile**. A simile compares one thing to another by using the words **like** or **as**. Here are some more examples:

- I am as hungry **as** a bear today!
- Watch out, she's **like** a monster!
- He's **as** slippery as a seal.

Metaphors and similes are tools to help you make your writing more creative.

Now it's your turn to practice writing **metaphors**. The first two are examples for you:

- The baby is a wiggly worm.
- His feet were two giant boulders.

Your hair is _____

My friend is _____

The rain was _____

Now try some **similes**. The first two are examples for you:

- The sun is **as** round **as** an orange.
- The baby's toes are **like** peas in a pod.

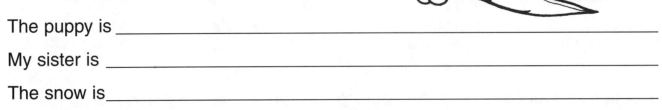

The puppy is _____

My sister is _____

The snow is_____

Challenge: Write a story using at least one metaphor and one simile to describe someone or something.

For Younger Students: Write some examples of similes and metaphors on the board to introduce the concept to students. Then have them brainstorm more and choose their favorites to write on a blank piece of paper and illustrate. These will make an interesting wall display.

Time to Write a Sloppy Copy

You will never have a finished story if you don't start with a sloppy copy. A **sloppy copy** is like an artist's sketch or a potter's lump of clay. You have to start somewhere, so start with something that looks like messy lines or a lumpy clump of shapeless clay. Then, shape it into something wonderful. You need words on paper before you can start to shape them into something wonderful. A sloppy copy is your first draft. A first draft is everything you can think of that you want to say in your story. Here are some tips for writing your first draft:

1. Just write.
2. Don't worry about spelling or punctuation.
3. Just write.
4. Let your ideas flow, and keep writing.
5. Get as much of your story down as you can.
6. Fix the spelling and grammar later.
7. Just write.
8. Make sure you can read your own writing.
9. Skip lines so you can add changes later.
10. Don't go too fast. You will forget important ideas.
11. Just write!

Many authors like to make outlines for their story ideas. Fill in the blanks below to plan your short story.

Plot Plan Outline

Setting (where and when the story happens)_____

_____

Characters (the people or animals in the story) _____

_____

Somebody wanted _____

so _____

but_____

so _____

Finally _____

Writer's Workshop

After you have a rough draft, or "sloppy copy," it's time for a writer's workshop. In the writer's workshop, you get to meet with other writers and take turns reading your stories. The other writers will ask questions about your story and let you know if your idea is good or if it needs more work. If it's just a sloppy copy, it will need more work. You and the other writers will want to meet in a writer's workshop after your second, and maybe even your third, draft as well. This is the time when writers help each other as they shape their stories. Here are some things to remember about a writer's workshop:

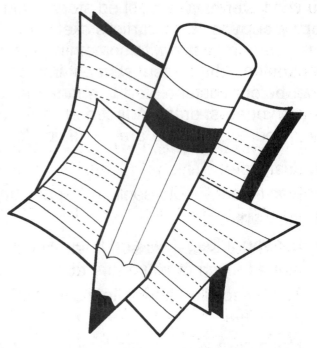

1. Be kind and polite. Everyone else is as nervous as you are about reading their stories in front of others.

2. Talk about what you don't understand about another story, if it confused you. And be sure to tell what you like about each story.

3. Bring paper and a pen or pencil to the writer's workshop. You might want to take some notes while another author is reading so you can help that author. And you will really want to take notes when others talk about your story.

4. Listen carefully when other writers are reading their stories.

5. Listen carefully when other writers are talking about your story.

6. Think about the things that the others say about your story. You may not use all the advice you are given, but there is sure to be lots of good advice that you can use.

7. Thank the other writers for helping you with your story. Plan to meet again after you have each had time to edit your stories.

42

Put on Your Editor's Hat

You can't be two different people at once, and it's not a good idea to try to be a creative writer and an editor at the same time. When you are being a creative writer, you are just writing. You are not stopping to correct your spelling or punctuation. You are not worried about that because you have an editor who will fix all of your mistakes. And who is your editor? You! When you are finished being a creative writer, you can start being an editor. Here's how:

1. **Pretend that you have never seen your story before.** Put your story away for a while before editing. This will allow you to completely change from being a creative writer to being an editor. You will be a better editor and find more of the things that really need to be changed.

2. **Read the story aloud.** If you can read it aloud to your family or friends, even better. You will be able to tell if it is clear or confusing, smooth or bumpy. You will be able to tell if you said what you wanted to write. Have a pencil handy so you can circle the parts you want to change.

3. **Start making changes.** This is called **revising**. When you make changes, read them aloud to see if you like them. You may want to change them again or put them back the way the were. Not every change is a good one. The more you practice the better you'll become.

4. **Check to see if you used dialogue**. Stories are more interesting when your characters talk to each other.

5. **Revise some more**. Take out any words that don't need to be there. Check again for spelling, punctuation, and grammar mistakes. If you're not sure about a word, look it up.

6. **Get some feedback**. Have a friend read your story to see if there is anything else that needs to be changed. Take your story to a writer's workshop and see what others think.

Writer's Checklist

When you have a final copy, it's time for one last check. Before you turn in your story, use this checklist to be sure it is ready:

_____ Did you include a setting in your story?

_____ Is there a problem for your main character in your story?

_____ Does your main character (protagonist) seem like he or she is real?

_____ Is your story interesting?

_____ Have you used any of the five senses in your story?

_____ Did you remember to "show" and not "tell"?

_____ Have you checked the spelling and grammar?

_____ Have you read the story aloud to be sure that it makes sense?

Story Starters

Cut out these story starters and place them in a small container or envelope. When you need a story idea, you can pull out a story starter to get your story started. Try using the same story starter more than once and write a different story each time. Write some more story starters to add to these.

Lindsay was so happy with her new puppy. She named him "Pookie" and she was teaching him to shake hands and roll over. He was just a fluffy ball of fur, and he liked to give her doggie kisses all over her face. She hurried home from school each day to play with Pookie, but one day the puppy wasn't there.

My mom told me to take a box of cookies to my grandma's house around the corner. I put them in the basket of my bicycle and started pedaling. As soon as I got to the end of the street, I saw the Dawson brothers, the neighborhood bullies, standing there with their arms folded and looking really mean.

David walked home from school very slowly. His friends were laughing and running around, but David just kept walking. He watched his toes step onto the sidewalk over and over again. When he finally got home, he trudged up the front porch steps, and there stood his mother watching him. "What's wrong with you?" she asked.

Our neighbors' tree grew so big that it came right over our fence. One day I was looking at it and decided that I could climb it. I grabbed the lowest branch and pulled myself up to the trunk and then kept climbing until I got to the top. You wouldn't believe what I saw!

Story Starters *(cont.)*

"Hello, Sweet Potato!" My grandma always calls me that when I visit, and then she tells me to climb into her lap. This time when I went to visit, she said, "Hello, Jason." I was so surprised. I stood there and didn't say anything for a while, and then I asked her if she wanted me to climb into her lap.

I was standing outside, waiting for my brother to come home when a very strange and mysterious thing happened. A little lady was walking down the street, carrying a brown paper sack. When she got to me, she said, "Here," and handed me the sack. I looked at the sack in my hands, and when I looked up, I couldn't see the lady anywhere! I started to look inside...

Cassie and Adam stood and looked at the seashore. Their parents were inside, unpacking for their usual vacation at the beach. Cassie and Adam thought it would be boring, as usual. Then they saw the pirates.

I went to the store to get some bread for dinner. I was looking everywhere for the bread when I backed into a tower of cereal boxes. They all came down on top of me, and then I heard a voice saying, "What are you doing here, under all these cereal boxes?"

My best friend is such a klutz. I like him a lot, but he is so clumsy. It seems like we can't go anywhere without a lot of excitement. The other day we were at the skating rink. We were just going to skate for a while and then go to my little sister's birthday party. We ended up being there until after dark. It all started when...

Mallory was sitting on the beach while Kendra waded in the shallow water. A man with a long, white beard walked by, handed something to Kendra, and then walked on. Kendra ran up to Mallory, "Did you see the old man with the long beard? He gave me this sand dollar, and it has something written on it." Together they held it in their hands and read.

Publishing

Are you a published author yet? Published authors have their stories in newspapers, magazines, and books, but there are other ways to be published too.

Publishing your story means putting it in a form that can be shared with others. For example, write your story and:

- mail it to a friend.
- include it in your portfolio.
- give it to someone as a gift.

- have it posted on the bulletin board.
- include it in a class collection of stories.
- send it to everyone you know by e-mail.

If you would like to try to get your story published in a magazine so even more people can read it, you can try the magazines below. These magazines publish stories written by kids just like you.

Cricket Magazine
Carus Publishing
315 Fifth Street
Peru, IL 61354-0300
(800) 827-0227

Jack and Jill &
Children's Digest
1100 Waterway Blvd.
Indianapolis, IN 46206
(800) 444-2704

Highlights for Children
Attention: Our Own Stories
803 Church Street
Honesdale, PA 18431
(570) 253-1080
*Stories should be 200 words or less

Stone Soup
Attention: Editor
P.O. Box 83
Santa Cruz, CA 95063
(800) 447-4569
*Include self-addressed, stamped envelope (SASE).

For more information take a look at the book *Market Guide for Young Writers* by Kathy Henderson (Shoe Tree Press, 1990).

Answer Key

Page 23

Cinderella—Goodness brings the best things in life.

Beauty and the Beast—Don't judge a book by its cover.

Pinocchio—Honesty is the best choice.

Page 25

Fairy Tale Plot:

1. The wicked stepsisters prevent her from going to the ball.
2. Her fairy godmother rescues her and sends her to the ball.
3. The prince finds her when her foot fits the glass slipper.

Adventure Plot:

1. The class wants to take a hot air balloon trip, but it will cost a lot of money.
2. They recycle lots of newspapers, cans, and bottles.
3. They get to go on their adventure. They have a great time!

Page 26

The Three Little Pigs—the wolf

Cinderella—the wicked stepmother and stepsisters

Sleeping Beauty—the witch

101 Dalmatians—Cruella DeVil

Hansel and Gretel—the witch living in the gingerbread house

Little Red Riding Hood—the wolf

Page 33

Answers will vary, but here are some ideas:

	Nasty	Nice
To a new boy at school	"You can't play."	"Come play with us."
To someone who has just offered an invitation to a party	"I don't want to go!"	"Thank you very much!"
To the substitute teacher	"I don't have to listen to you!"	"Can I help you?"
To a parent who has said it's time for bed	"No!"	"Okay."
To the teacher who says it's time to put away the equipment	"Ah...do we have to?"	"I'll go get the baseballs!"

Page 36

The circled items are listed below. All others should be underlined.

2. There was a tall, blue vase full of bright, purple irises on the table.
4. Maria saw a tiny, white dog with muddy paws and a nervous tail.
6. I saw Mr. Olsen buy lunch for Lanni after Joey sat on hers.
9. My cat sounds like an engine starting when she purrs.
12. Her hair is the color of a tortilla before it is cooked.
14. That car is the color of pistachio ice cream.

Page 40

Answers will vary, but here are metaphors:

Your hair is (spaghetti, a rat's nest, etc.).

My friend is (a squeaky mouse, a ferocious lion, a grumpy bear, etc.).

The rain was (fierce tears, a waterfall, etc.).

Similes:

The puppy is (like a wiggly fuzz ball, like a stuffed animal, etc.).

My sister is (like a tiger, like a butterfly, etc.).

The snow is (like marshmallow creme, cotton balls, etc.)